The PUP

SHOW

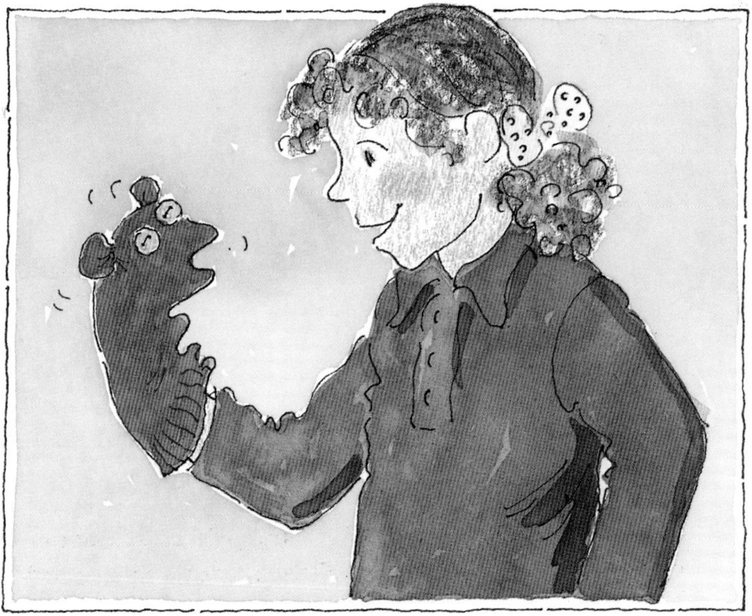

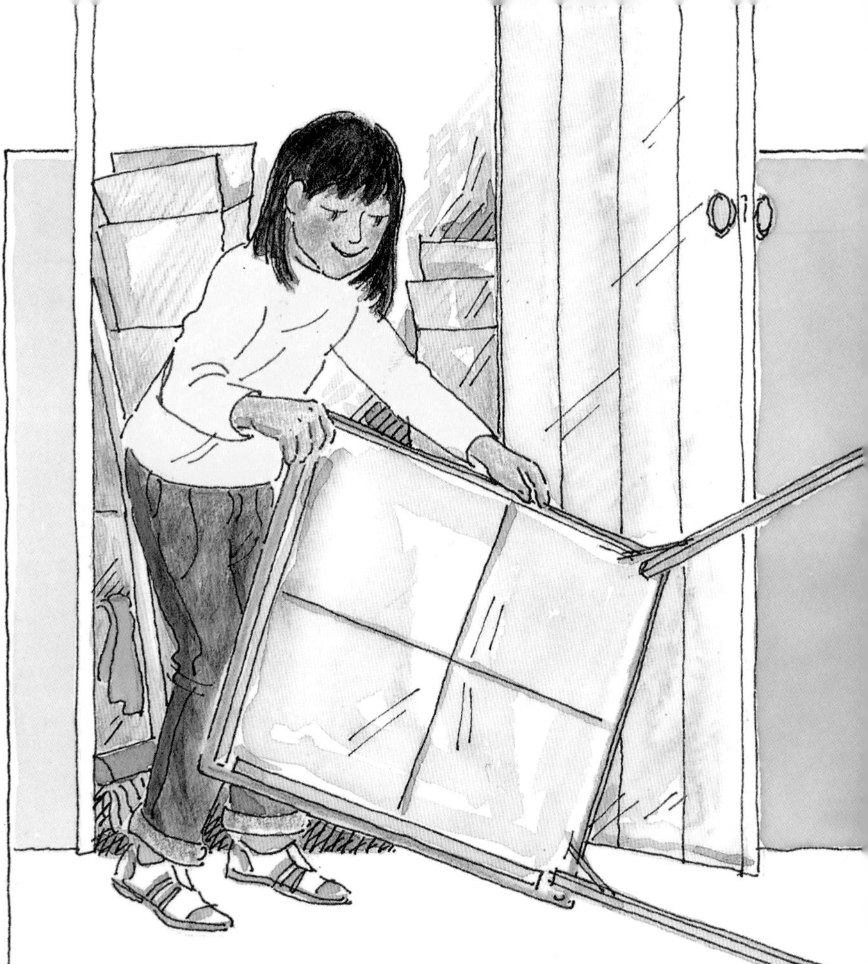

Find a table

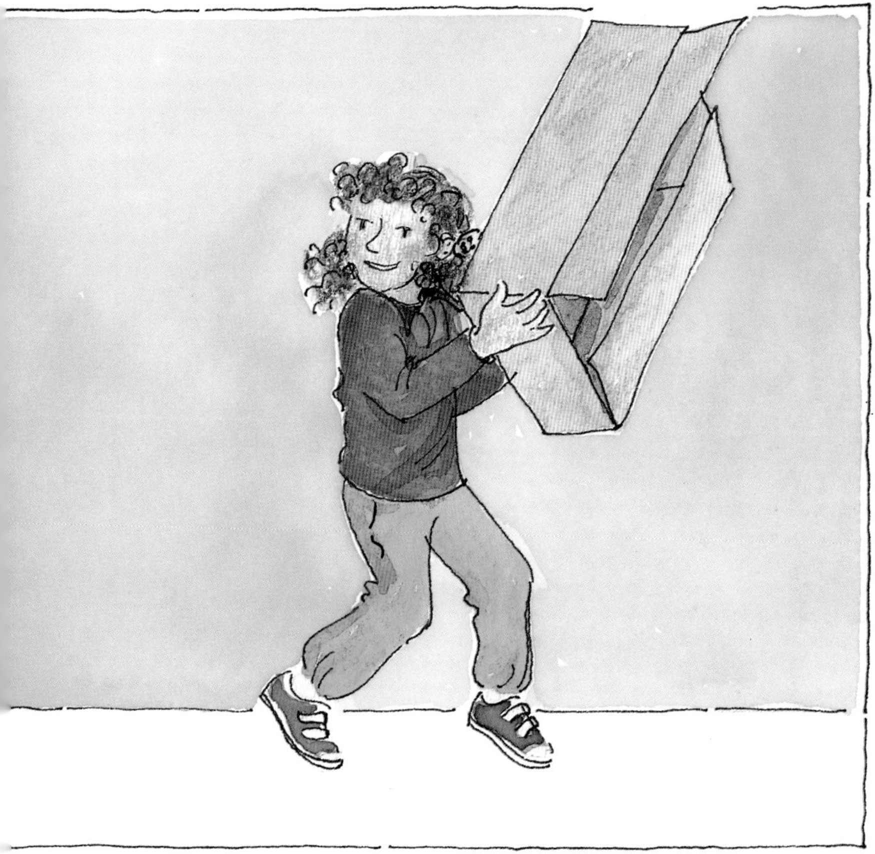

and a box.

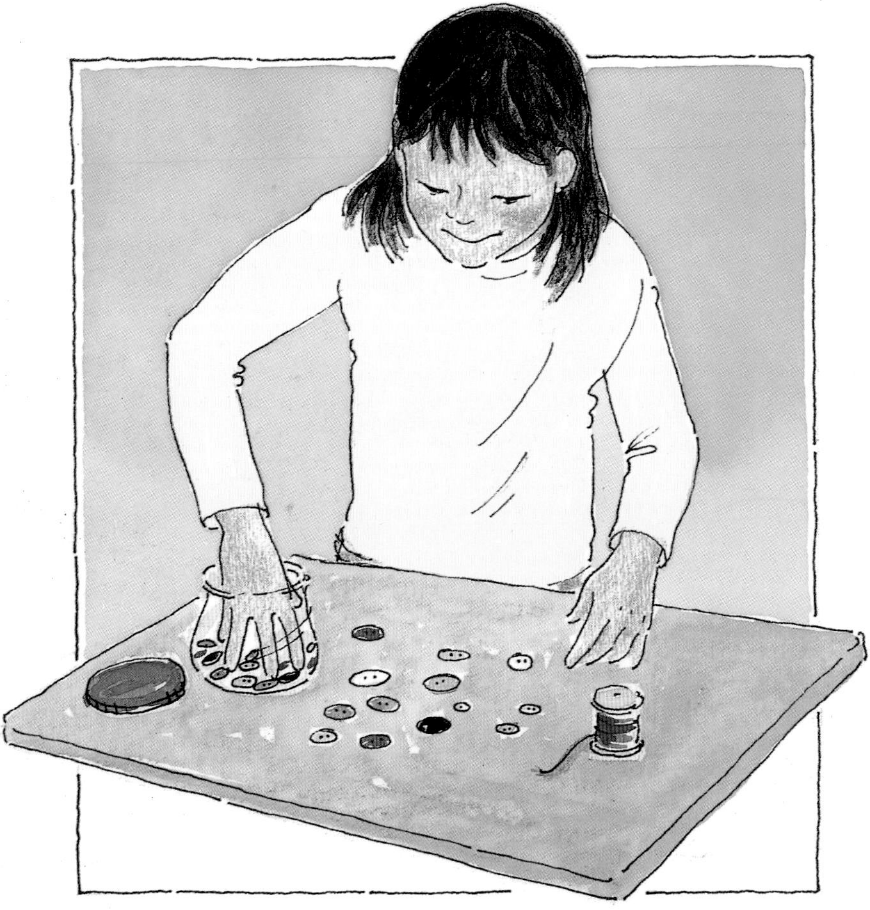

Find some buttons

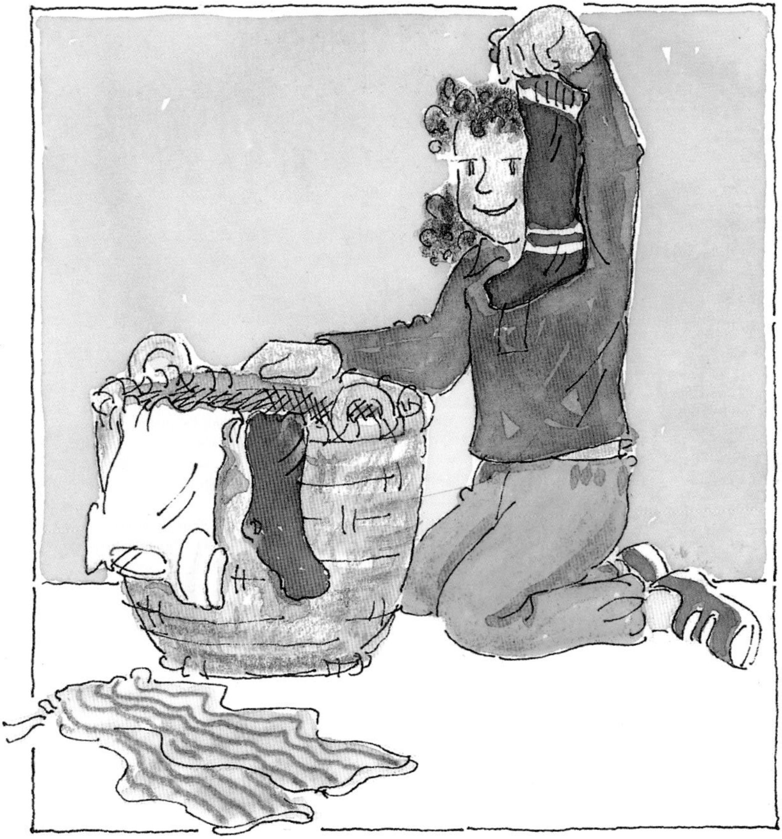

and some socks.

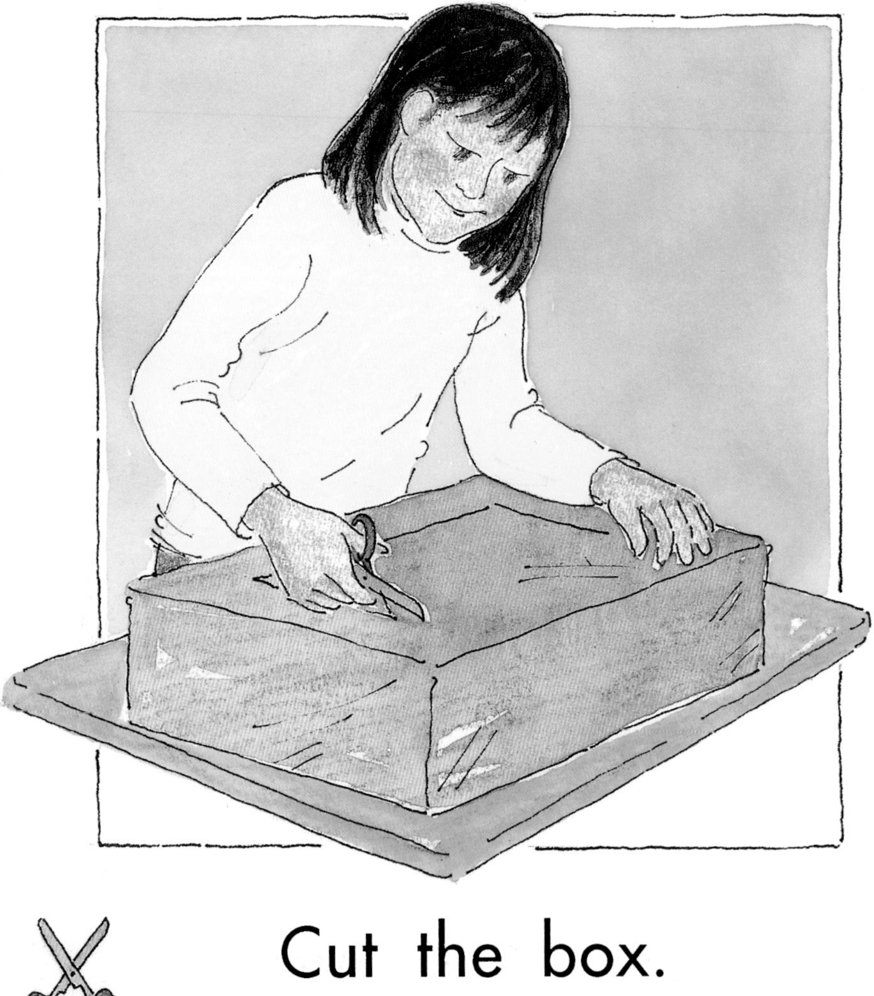

Cut the box.

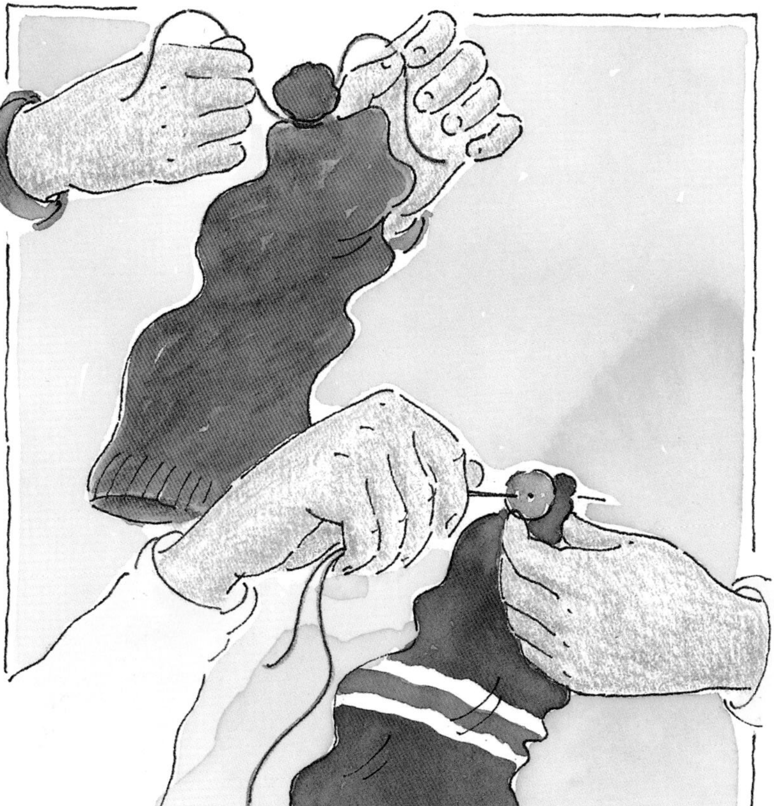

Twist and sew.

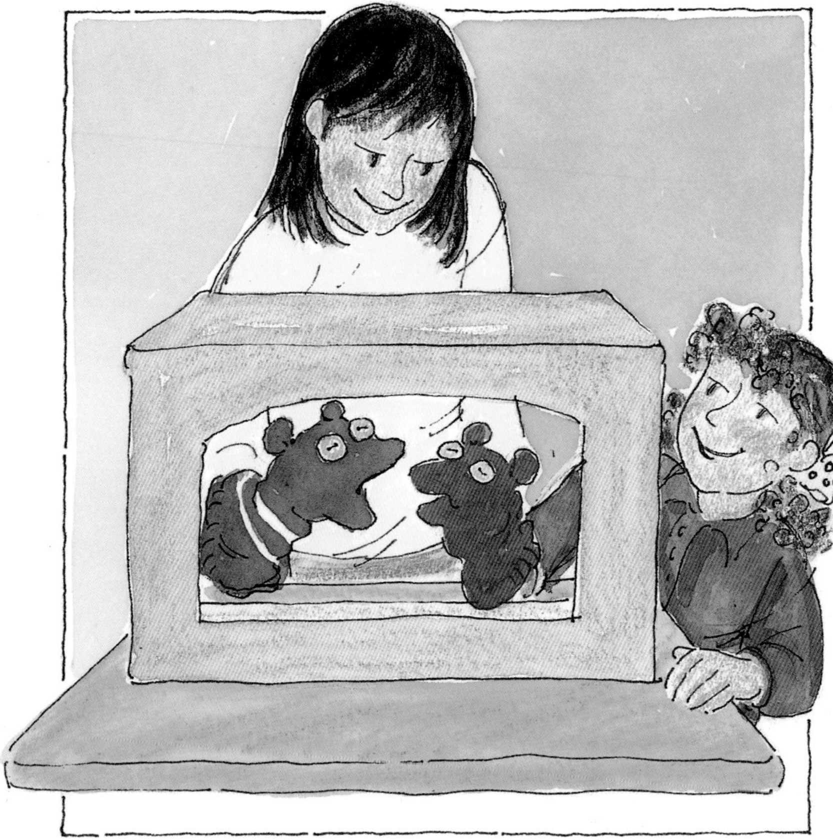

Now you can have
a puppet show.